MODEL MAN

Study Guide

Bethany Publishing

Cover Design by: Cameron Roberson

Edited by: Brenda Pitts

For Worldwide Distribution, Printed in the U.S.A.

1 2 3 4 5 6 7 8 / 19 18 17 16 15

MODEL MAN

Study Guide

LARRY STOCKSTILL

CONTENTS

How to Use This Guide

Group Size

A group of eight men is perfect for using this Model Man study guide. This group can be easily accommodated around a large table or in a living room setting. If the group is larger, such as a Sunday school class or other large gathering, it can be divided as needed. Even groups of four to six men will work fine.

Time Frame

The entire meeting should last no more than an hour. The first 10 to 15 minutes are set aside for fellowship and interaction. Then the 20-minute video is played. The last 25 to 30 minutes is reserved for discussion and prayer.

Scope and Sequence

Each of the six video lessons covers one or two chapters of the *Model Man* book. We recommend that the appropriate chapters be read by each group member the week of, and prior to, the meeting.

Group Facilitator

Each group should be facilitated by a leader. The role of the leader is not to teach but to direct the flow of response by group members. Each week the facilitator prepares in advance for each session, starts the DVD lesson, and directs the group toward a time of ministry at the end. It is also his responsibility to be sure the meeting ends after one hour. If further ministry is desired, it can take place after the meeting is adjourned.

Instructions for the Lessons

1. **Video:** Show the 20-minute video and fill in the blanks in the lesson as it plays.

2. **Discussion:** Use the next 15 to 20 minutes to lead the group through the discussion questions.

3. **Ministry time:** Reserve the last 10 minutes for a time of prayer and ministry, using the ministry points provided.

4. **Self-study:** These points provide for further private study in the Bible and correspond with the primary theme discussed in the lesson. This study can be done at home during the week following the meeting to enhance the principles learned in the meeting.

5. **Action points:** Each lesson ends with action points that the leader should read together with the group. This solidifies the commitments each person must make in order to see life changes.

SESSION

1

Integrity

Listed below are the main points of video 1. As the video plays, fill in the blanks as that information is provided. Answers are included at the back of this guide.

I. *Integrity* means "whole, with no part missing."

A. *"A good name is more desirable than great riches"* (Proverbs 22:1 NIV).

B. Having integrity means having the courage to do the right thing, to live by standards, principles, conscience, and conviction 100 percent of the time.

II. Integrity has three parts.

A. A man of integrity tells the ________________.

1. A lie is the intent to ________________, whether it is a half-truth (withholding important facts) or an exaggeration (embellishing the truth with false statements).

2. It is important to tell the truth to everyone, but particularly to your ________________ and your employer.

B. A man of integrity keeps his ________________.

1. Your word is your ________________.

2. Integrity is making promises and ________________ those promises.

C. A man of integrity pays his ________________.

1. Finances tell more about your integrity than anything else.

2. Paying your ________________ and your ________________ means that you are showing integrity toward both God and your nation.

3. Faithfulness to your ________________ in little things, like expense reports and removing items from your workplace, is true integrity.

4. We must be careful to handle funds ________________.

Discussion Questions

1. *Integrity* means "whole, with no part missing." It is conducting yourself with honesty, faithfulness, and financial accuracy. In your observations of the people in your business or profession, which area of integrity seems to be the hardest to keep?

____

____

____

____

____

2. A lie is the intent to deceive. Have you ever been tempted to withhold information to get a sale or to exaggerate the claims of a product in order to close a deal? Have you ever withheld information from your wife or employer to keep from looking bad?

3. *Your word is your bond.* A generation ago, this phrase meant anything that came out of your mouth became your commitment. What has changed about that concept in business? In marriage? In everyday

promises? Discuss how easy it is to say things without thinking and to never fulfill them.

4. Paying your bills on time helps not only your *credit* rating but also your *credibility* rating. What pattern have you established to help you ensure that all your bills are paid in a timely way? What is your biggest challenge in keeping bills up to date?

5. It's very easy to be loose with the property of others. Has the Lord dealt with you about an item, large or small, that actually belongs to your company but is presently in your possession? How about something you borrowed from your neighbor that you have never returned? How could that be affecting your integrity?

Ministry Time

1. Lying and deception reveal a deep insecurity. It is a fear that if we are totally honest and transparent, we will be rejected. It often comes from a lack of affirmation from a father. If being 100 percent truthful has been a battle for you, allow the group to pray over you and ask the Lord to heal that wound.

2. We all want to please others and thus make statements that we end up not keeping: "I'll call you later today," or "I'll be home at 5:00 for dinner," or "We will take that product back if it doesn't work for you." Perhaps you have seen that pattern in your life. Ask the group to pray for you that your word would be your bond and that whatever comes out of your mouth to your wife, kids, friends, or coworkers would be something you honor.

3. When we are late paying bills and maintaining financial commitments, it is usually the result of a lack of order. Things are out of place, bills are disorganized, and we lose track of what we owe. Who

in the group would like prayer that their finances would come back into order and that the result would be a higher credit score and greater borrowing power?

4. Divide into pairs and share with each other the most difficult part of integrity for you (truthfulness, keeping your promises, paying your bills, etc.). Then pray for each other for God to change you into a model man in that area.

Self-Study

The Bible is full of amazing characters who exemplified integrity. Look up these characters and see which ones apply to you.

1. *Job: Integrity in Adversity*

> *"Have you considered my servant Job, that there is none like him on the earth, a blameless and upright man, who fears God and turns away from evil? He still holds fast his* ***integrity,*** *although you incited me against him to*

destroy him without reason" (Job 2:3, emphasis added).

2. *Abraham: Integrity in Obedience*

"I am God Almighty; walk before Me, and be blameless [have integrity]*"* (Genesis 17:1, NASB).

3. *Daniel: Integrity in Finances*

"They could find no ground for complaint or any fault, because he was faithful, and no error or fault was found in him" (Daniel 6:4).

The Bible is also full of characters whose integrity was not whole. They paid a price for small deceptions.

1. *Achan: Theft of Holy Things*

"Israel has sinned; they have transgressed my covenant that I commanded them; they have taken some of the devoted things; they have stolen and lied and put them among their own belongings" (Joshua 7:11).

2. *Gehazi: Deception about Receiving*

"'Where have you been, Gehazi?' And he said, 'Your servant went nowhere'" (2 Kings 5:25).

3. *Ananias and Sapphira: Deception about Giving*

"Why is it that you have contrived this deed in your heart? You have not lied to men but to God" (Acts 5:4).

Action Points

1. *I will be a man of truth.* I will speak the truth 100 percent of the time. No deception, no half-truths, no exaggeration, and regardless of the embarrassment, I will speak the truth.

2. *I will be a man of my word.* Whatever comes out of my mouth is my bond. Even if it costs me time, money, and influence, I will honor what I have said to God and to others as supreme. I will live my life by principle and without regard to personalities.

3. *I will have financial integrity.* I will be a man who pays his bills promptly, honors all his financial commitments, returns borrowed or stolen merchandise, and handles all money with transparency and accountability to others.

SESSION

2

PURITY AND EXAMPLE

LISTED BELOW ARE the main points of video 2. As the video plays, fill in the blanks as that information is provided. Answers are included at the back of this guide.

I. Purity

A. ______________ followed three rules as a Nazarite.

1. *Never touch a grape.* What was Samson doing in a vineyard?

2. *Never touch a dead body.* What was Samson doing with his hand inside the carcass of a lion?

3. *Never cut your hair.* After breaking the first two standards, it was easy for Samson to lay his head in Delilah's lap and get his hair cut.

B. Here are some simple standards of purity to follow.

1. *Never be* ________________ *with a woman* (Billy Graham, the Modesto Manifesto).

2. *Watch the* ________________ *gate* (King David looking out over the rooftops of Jerusalem and seeing Bathsheba).

3. *Always be* ________________ *for where you are.* We all do better when we are watched.

4. *Travel with* ________________ *if possible.* Jesus set the example of sending out His disciples two by two.

5. *Filter your* ________________. The Internet is the most dangerous weapon of lust in Satan's arsenal.

6. *Control your* ________________. Some cable channels show full-blown pornography after 11:00 P.M.

7. *Be on guard in your* ________________. Most workplaces have those who are seeking to get out of a bad marriage or to snag a husband.

8. *Be aware of the progression of adultery.* First comes a look, then a touch, an embrace, a kiss, and finally full-blown adultery.

II. Example

A. "*Brothers, join in imitating me, and keep your eyes on those who walk according to the* ________________ *you have in us*" (Phil. 3:17).

B. *Be an example in your* ________________. Controlling the tongue is the most difficult part of being an example, particularly in high-pressure situations.

C. *Be an example in your* ________________. Follow the rules set up to protect society, controlling your emotions in stressful situations (particularly on the highway!).

D. *Be an example in* ________________. Live a life of order and organization, not confusion and chaos.

This applies to all areas of your life—closets, car, yard, clothes, punctuality, etc.

E. *Be an example in your* ________________. Set an example for others in how to honor and treat a wife with respect.

F. *Be an example in your* ________________. Having children who are respectful and submitted to their parents is a powerful example for others to imitate.

Discussion Questions

1. One of the illustrations in the video was of a worm that lures its prey with a blinking light, then captures it and eats it. How is that illustration appropriate to the lustful eyes of a man toward an attractive female who is not his wife? Discuss how the progressive nature of an affair is similar to the moth becoming gradually stuck until it is helpless.

____

____

____

2. Why do we need guidelines and non-negotiables for purity? Discuss Billy Graham's guideline to never be alone with a woman and why that is critical in lunches, carpools, office meetings, travel, and other settings.

3. Jesus sent His workers out two by two. Why is it important that you make yourself accountable for where you are and whom you are with?

4. Media (Internet and cable TV) have become huge sources of temptation for men, with media companies becoming more and more creative on how to get images in front of your eyes even without your consent. Discuss the steps you have taken (or need to take) to keep your eyes from roving like David's and to protect the environment in your home for your benefit and for your children's protection as well.

5. What situation causes you to lose it more than any other? Is it in a store, on the highway, or at work? How can you protect yourself from becoming a bad Christian example to others who are watching?

6. If the group checked out your car, your garage, and your closets today, what would they find? Is the confusion of your environment discounting the witness of your mouth?

Ministry Time

1. Pair up with one other man and ask each other this simple question: In what place, time, or setting do you feel most vulnerable to sexual temptation? Pray for each other to set up guidelines and for the strength of the Holy Spirit to overcome sexual temptation.

2. In the same setting of one-on-one prayer and ministry, discuss this second question: What behavior in your speech or conduct is not a good example of a Christian to the lost and to your own family?

3. For group ministry, pray together for God to change your character to be a model of integrity, purity, and example in your family and workplace.

Self-Study

Who are some of the people in the Bible who allowed their sexual desires to destroy their lives, families, and example?

1. David (2 Samuel 11)

- David was in the midlife season of his life and was rich, successful, and powerful. He became bored with his success, and Satan made sure to put an image directly in front of him that he could not resist.
- We all need to guard ourselves against depression, fatigue, and even success. These

are seasons when we are most vulnerable to sexual temptation.

- A good offense is the best defense. When your marriage is exciting and intimate, you are far less subject to sexual temptation.

- David's adultery led him on a trail of manipulation, cover-up, and ultimately the murder of Bathsheba's husband. Be open and accountable to another Christian brother the moment you sense a temptation toward a woman who is not your wife.

2. *Amnon (2 Samuel 13:1-15)*

- Amnon's lust drew him to his half-sister Tamar. He fantasized about her day and night. Fantasy is the seedbed of adultery. Never allow your mind to project images of possible scenes of sexual pleasure.

- His cousin Jonadab suggested a plan of how he could get Tamar into his bed (v. 5). Your friendships with ungodly men have a powerful influence on your behavior. You must walk in the counsel of the godly.

- After Amnon's rape of his half-sister (v. 14), *"the hatred with which he hated her was greater than the love with which he had loved her"* (v. 15). Always remember that lust wants to throw away what it has used. It is not based on love, faithfulness, loyalty, and commitment but is short-term, seasonal, and destroys every life that it touches.

Who is a person in the Bible who exemplifies sexual purity?

1. Joseph (Genesis 39:6-12)

- Joseph was *"handsome in form and appearance"* (v. 6). His looks naturally attracted women. If you happen to be handsome, women will let you know that and will often do anything possible to find their way into an intimate relationship with you.
- Potiphar's wife *"spoke to Joseph day after day"* (v. 10). However, Joseph "would not listen to her" (v. 10). Be careful of the little looks, little flirts, little text messages, small innuendoes of seduction. When a relationship like this is progressing, you must seek strength,

counsel, and partnership from other Christian men who are pure.

- *"He left his garment in her hand and fled and got out of the house"* (v. 12). *Flee* a dangerous relationship. Change your phone number if necessary. Change jobs if necessary. Change cities if necessary! Nothing is worth sacrificing the purity and example of your life. Joseph's example was that of a man who called on the Holy Spirit to help him physically remove himself from the words, touch, and suggestions of an adulteress.

Action Points

1. *I will be a man of purity.* I will set up standards and guidelines, make myself accountable for my time and travel, and flee from the very appearance of evil.

2. *I will be an example in my community.* I will be a man who guards his tongue and emotions when in public. I will seek to honor the rules and regulations of law and business. I will keep my environment

and home orderly and organized as an example to the lost of what has changed in my life as a believer.

SESSION

3

The Pace of Grace

LISTED BELOW ARE the main points of video 3. As the video plays, fill in the blanks as that information is provided. Answers are included at the back of this guide.

I. Your Yoke

A. There is a huge difference between *drive* and being ________________.

B. I used to work *for* God; now I work ________________ God.

C. Your yoke is your ________________.

D. *"Take my yoke upon you, and learn from me, for I am gentle and lowly in heart, and you will find rest for your souls. For my yoke is easy, and my burden is light"* (Matt. 11:29-30). ________________ will give you rest.

II. Your Inner Circle

A. Don't try to ________________, prioritize, and prop up everyone in the world.

B. The center of your circle is your ________________.

C. The next level of your inner circle is your ________________.

D. The third part of your inner circle is your spiritual sons, those you are mentoring. Some people ________________ your time; some people ________ your time.

E. The final, most outer part of your circle is made up of boards, committees, and any other commitments you have made.

III. Your Money

A. You manage money with ________________.

B. Don't live off the bottom of the barrel; live off the ________________ of the barrel.

C. Live by the 10/10/80 principle: tithe 10 percent, save 10 percent, and live on ________________ percent.

IV. Your Opportunities

A. Not every opportunity is from God. It is important that you ________________ about every opportunity.

B. The devil gives revolving doors; God gives __________ doors.

V. Your Discipline

A. Discipline is the ability to maintain a ________________. If your schedule is unrealistic, you will never maintain it.

B. Start with daily devotions. Time spent alone with the Lord is not wasting your time but it is ________________ your time.

C. Next is your work schedule. You should try not to work over ________________ hours a week.

D. Third is your family schedule. You need a family night and a date night every week. You need a ________________ every year.

E. Next is your health schedule.

1. Rest: Try to get ________________ hours of sleep a night.

2. Exercise: Because you are losing ________________ of your muscle mass every year, you need to exercise and work out.

3. Diet: Change your diet to eating like a ________________ for breakfast, like a prince for lunch, and like a pauper for supper. Be careful of that voice at 10:30 at night that says, "Long live the king!"

Discussion Questions

1. Jesus said, *"My yoke is easy"*; however, our yoke is hard! What are some of the things that contribute to our adrenaline-driven, ego-driven schedules that we try to maintain? Was Moses' father-in-law right that Moses would have worn himself out if he had continued in his current pace?

2. We all try to please everyone, and we end up pleasing no one. Discuss how your wife and family always seem to get the leftovers of your schedule and life instead of being the center of your life.

3. Managing money is all about margins. What kind of financial margins have you set to keep from living in a continual crisis? Give some testimonies of how tithing and saving have changed your financial picture.

4. Have you ever had a seemingly golden opportunity turn out to be a nightmare? Did you pray about the opportunity beforehand, or did you just take it because you thought an opportunity like this would come along only once in a lifetime?

5. Go around the circle and let every man say at least one change he needs to make to his schedule—devotions, work hours, family time, sleep hours, exercise time, or daily diet.

Ministry Time

1. Our ego can be the driver that is destroying us. We want to impress, to achieve, to outdo others because of a lack of affirmation. Ask the group to pray for you if you have always been a workaholic and feel it may be tied to a lack of affirmation from a father who demanded more from you and never validated your efforts.

2. Have your wife and children suffered from neglect because you were more focused on pleasing people at work? Ask the group to pray for you that you could get your family back in order and moved back to the bull's-eye of your priorities.

3. Financial pressure destroys our health. It can come from the loss of a job, a health challenge, or perhaps from failing to tithe and save. If you are facing tremendous financial pressure right now, ask the group to pray for a breakthrough and for the ability to live with the proper margins.

4. Pair up with another man in the group and share with him your greatest challenge in your schedule. Pray together for God to give you the discipline you need to implement a direct change in your devotional life, family time, work schedule, diet, sleep, or exercise.

Self-Study

Pride is a driver. It forces us to take on challenges and responsibilities just to prove our worth. Here are a few Bible examples.

1. ***Saul was at one time a very humble man, even though he was "head and shoulders taller than anyone else in the land"* (1 Sam. 9:2 NLT).**

- Later on, however, when he had been king for a while, his pride and ego turned to rebellion.

  "When you were little in your own eyes, were you not head of the tribes of Israel? …Why then did you not obey the voice of the Lord?" (1 Samuel 15:17,19 NKJV).

2. ***Uzziah was a great king before the Lord* (2 Chron. 26).**

   - *"As long as he sought the Lord, God made him prosper"* (v. 5).
   - At the end of his life, however, he egotistically forced his way into the temple to offer incense, and *"leprosy broke out on his forehead in the presence of the priests in the house of the Lord"* (v. 19).

3. ***Satan was cast out of heaven because of ego and pride.***

   - We must be sure that our ego is not driving us into areas and assignments that we have not been given from the Lord.

The principle of the *inner circle* involves delegation. It means that you don't try to do the whole job by yourself. We can see this principle at work in two very important spiritual persons in the Bible.

1. ***Moses: God told Moses to delegate his ministry to seventy elders and rulers of thousands, hundreds, fifties, and tens*** **(Exod. 18:21).**

    - This one shift in his ministry established the government of Israel for thousands of years and enabled Moses to step back into the pace of grace.

2. ***Jesus: Jesus had an inner circle.***

    - The Lord prayed all night and then selected twelve of His disciples *"so that they might be with him and he might send them out to preach"* (Mark 3:14).

    - He also empowered seventy other disciples, whom He sent out in pairs into every village to which He would go (see Luke 11).

Living with *margins* means a surplus is prepared for every possible scenario.

In the Bible, the greatest example of living with margins is Joseph.

- Instead of consuming all the grain in the seven years of plenty, Joseph set up margins for the nation: *"Let Pharaoh...take one-fifth of the produce of the land of Egypt during the seven plentiful years"* (Genesis. 41:34).
- This 20 percent sustained Egypt during the awful seven years of famine so that they had food when no one else in the entire world did. If we tithe 10 percent and save 10 percent (a total of 20 percent), God will sustain us through any difficult time that may be approaching in the future.

Opportunities may be from the Lord, or they may be a deception of the enemy.

In the Bible, Joshua was fooled by a deception that looked like an opportunity.

- He looked at the old clothing and moldy bread of the Gibeonites and believed their story about being from a far country. He entered into a covenant with them, not knowing that they were actually part of the tribes in Palestine that God had told His people to destroy.

> *"So the men took some of their provisions, but did not ask counsel from the Lord"* (Joshua 9:14).

Our *schedule* should always start with time with God.

Jesus gave us a great example.

> *"And rising very early in the morning, while it was still dark, he departed and went out into a desolate place, and there he prayed"* (Mark 1:35).

Action Points

1. *I will walk in the yoke with Jesus.* I will not allow my ego or schedule to drive me. I will walk in the pace of grace.

2. *I will focus on my inner circle.* My wife, my children, and those I commit to mentor will receive the largest percentage of my focus and priority.

3. *I will maintain margins for my money.* I will faithfully tithe 10 percent and save 10 percent of all my income so that I can accumulate at least three months of my income in a savings account.

4. *I will pray about every opportunity, regardless of how amazing and fortunate it appears.* Through prayer, fasting, and counsel with my spouse and my advisers, I will proceed with any and every opportunity that I have discerned is an open door rather than a revolving door.

5. *I will maintain a disciplined schedule and lifestyle.* I will seek the Lord first in the morning, protect a weekly family night and date night, limit my work hours to fifty hours every week, practice a weekly Sabbath day and annual vacation for rest, and seek to rest, exercise, and eat in a disciplined way to maximize my health and years on the earth.

SESSION

4

PURPOSE

LISTED BELOW ARE the main points of video 4. As the video plays, fill in the blanks as that information is provided. Answers are included at the back of this guide.

I. The Meaning of Purpose

A. In a Harvard business school course, this question was asked: If you were dying and your granddaughter was sitting on the edge of your bed, what would you tell her is ________________ in life?

B. You should always go to the ________________ of life and work your way back. You cannot live a random life.

C. Purpose is about ________________. It is about finding your mission and remaining focused on it.

II. The "Two Trees" Illustration

A. The tree of ________________ building

1. This is a tree to climb the ladder of notoriety and popularity.

2. The branches in this tree are very small. People who get to the top usually find themselves falling.

3. The root of this tree is ________________.

B. The tree of ________________ God

1. Jesus said, *"I always do the things that are pleasing to him"* (John 8:29).

2. Paul said, *"Whether we are at home or away, we make it our aim to please him"* (2 Corinthians 5:9).

3. The root of that tree is ________________.

III. Three Words That Define Purpose

A. ____________

1. *Conviction* is something you do that you would die to defend. *Mandate* is something you do that you would die to accomplish.

2. Five billion people are not saved, and that line would circle the world thirty-seven times at the equator.

B. ____________

1. You need a plan, a method, a course of action.

2. Paul said, *"I do not account my life of any value nor as precious to myself, if only I may finish my course"* (Acts 20:24).

C. ____________

1. Money is not the most important thing in your purpose. What you need more than money is people.

2. "Pro-vision" comes from _______________.

Vision attracts resources to fulfill your vision.

3. Zacchaeus was in the tree of influence building. When he met Jesus, he changed trees to the tree of pleasing God and serving others. He volunteered to give half of his income to the poor and to repay fourfold anything he had stolen.

Discussion Questions

1. Go around the group and let each man answer this question: If you were dying and your granddaughter was sitting by you on the bed, what would you tell her should be her priority in life? How should that affect your living right now?

____

____

____

____

____

____

2. What are some of the ways we climb the tree of influence building? Have you known anyone who made it to the pinnacle of their career only to come crashing down in one day?

3. Jesus stayed in the tree of pleasing God. How does that tree set you free from impressing and imitating others? What area of serving others has given you the greatest fulfillment?

4. If you were to describe your personal mandate (what you would die to achieve), what would you say it is?

5. The story about the bushmaster snake had this ending: "When there is a big enough reason *why*, you

will always figure out the *how*." What purpose and passion is burning in your soul, but you just have not figured out a method to accomplish it?

Ministry Time

1. *Purpose* involves others. We can get so wrapped up in climbing the tree of influence that we lose all purpose and become totally self-focused. If your life has become totally wrapped up in accomplishing your career goals rather than in fulfilling the will of God for your life, ask the group to pray over you.

2. Perhaps you have had a piece of news recently that has shaken you, and you have started to reevaluate your priorities based upon that news. Share that news with the group and ask them to pray about those circumstances.

3. Satan knows that if he can attack your finances, he can attack your purpose. You can be a blessing to others only if you have been blessed! Ask the group to pray for you if financial challenges have put you into financial survival mode so that you are not able to do for others as you desire.

4. Zacchaeus experienced a total transformation of his purpose in one day. He gave half of his goods to the poor. Perhaps you have been deliberating doing something for others but lack the courage to obey your heart. Ask the group to pray for you that you would be able to step out and become a major blessing to something in line with your purpose.

Self-Study

Jesus demonstrates purpose more than any other Bible character. Here are a few outstanding moments in His life that illustrate that.

1. *"I must be about My Father's business"* (Luke 2:49 NKJV).

- Even at twelve years of age, Jesus already knew that He was destined to redeem the world. He was single-minded on preparing Himself for His destiny.

  Perhaps your purpose is something you have pursued since a young age. God has prepared you for "such a time as this" (Esther 4:14).

2. *"For this purpose I came to this hour"* (John 12:27 NASB).

- As Jesus' life drew to a close, He focused more and more on His death in Jerusalem. On the Mount of Transfiguration, He spoke with Moses and Elijah about His death. He even walked ahead of His disciples on the road leading to His death. He set His face like a flint to redeem mankind through the most horrible death ever devised by mankind—the cross.

- You may be walking through difficult times now. Does it have to do with your purpose, perhaps? Is the enemy trying to discourage you from accomplishing your mission? How can you take courage through Jesus' example?

Paul had a similar mandate and purpose upon His life.

1. ***He knew that he would be arrested and spend the rest of his life in prison when he went into Jerusalem.***

   "When we heard this, we and the people there urged him not to go up to Jerusalem. Then Paul answered, 'What are you doing, weeping and breaking my heart? For I am ready not only to be imprisoned but to die in Jerusalem for the name of the Lord Jesus'" (Acts 21:12-13).

2. ***Paul knew that His purpose was to go to Rome and testify before Caesar and that***

his ship could not go down before he accomplished that purpose.

"He said, 'Do not be afraid, Paul; you must stand before Caesar. And behold, God has granted you all those who sail with you.' So take heart, men, for I have faith in God that it will be exactly as I have been told" (Acts 27:24-25).

Action Points

1. I will not waste my life in the tree of influence building but will spend my life serving others in the tree of pleasing God.

2. I will live my life according to a personal mandate and prioritize that mandate over everything else I do.

3. God will help me to find a method that will enable me to fulfill that mandate.

4. My money and resources will simply be my tools to accomplish the mandate God has placed upon my life.

SESSION

5

FAMILY

LISTED BELOW ARE the main points of video 5. As the video plays, fill in the blanks as that information is provided. Answers are included at the back of this guide.

> *Husbands, live with your wives in an understanding way, showing honor to the woman as the weaker vessel, since they are heirs with you of the grace of life, so that your prayers may not be hindered* (1 Peter 3:7).

I. Seven Mistakes a Man Can Make with His Wife

A. Financial ________________

1. After the fall, God programmed a woman to feel vulnerable: *"Your desire will be for your husband, and he will rule over you"* (Geneses 3:16 NIV).

2. Women marry a man because they feel ________________ with him, not just because they are attracted to him.

3. Dave Ramsey, Christian financial expert, says that every couple needs ________________ ________________ of salary in the bank. This provides the security the wife needs to deal with future emergencies.

B. ________________

1. A woman supposedly speaks 25,000 words a day, and she has usually used up only 3,000 of them by the time her husband comes home. She has 22,000 words left that she wants to use on him!

2. The fact that you are living with your wife does not mean you are really *with* her. A woman can feel a lack of companionship even if you are in her physical company.

3. A woman wants to ________________ herself, not just unclothe herself. More than anything else, she wants to let you know who she is. That requires time to learn about her and appreciate her.

C. Lack of ________________

1. A woman feels upset if she does not have her husband in her home and in a routine. Interruptions can be a marriage's greatest enemy.

2. She looks forward to the little things you do together—morning exercise, breakfast, coffee, Bible reading, etc.

D. Lack of ________________

1. A woman wants to be able to talk to her husband about things that are bothering her about him. She is your greatest friend and ally and should be able to speak freely to you about anything.

2. *Never get defensive.* Your wife is not trying to attack you but to ________________ you. Just say *thank you* instead of turning it around and blaming all your character flaws on her.

E. ________________

1. Queen Elizabeth has been queen of England for sixty years and has not opened a door in public in those sixty years! She does not even have a driver's license. Men break their necks to accommodate her every need.

2. Walking beside your wife, standing up when she enters a room, opening a door ahead of her, and opening the car door for her all show your honor and respect for her.

3. Treat your wife like the ________________, and she will treat you like the king.

F. ________________

1. A wife is unhappy when she feels her husband is dishonest, deceptive, or manipulative. She feels mistrust if you flirt with waitresses and stewardesses and take your secretary to lunch.

2. Try to take the steps necessary so she never has the feeling of mistrust. *Never, never* lie to her or deceive her in any way.

G. ____________

1. If a woman feels that her husband would not step between her and danger, she feels unhappy. If she feels that if she got sick and was dying, her husband would not take care of her, she is unhappy.

2. Ruth said to Boaz, "____________ *me*" (see Ruth 3:9 NASB). That meant, "Step between me and any danger I face."

II. Raising Godly Children

A. ____________

1. Always know where your children are and whom they are with.

2. Spend fifteen minutes of quality time with each child every day.

B. ____________

1. Children need to hear you say, "I am proud of you."

2. Affirmation means that you will be present at their big days.

3. The problems in our world come down to a father who was ________________, anonymous, or abusive.

C. ________________

1. God put a boundary around the tree of the knowledge of good and evil in the Garden of Eden. He also told Adam and Eve the consequences of breaking that boundary.

2. The only thing that changes character is ________________. You hold all the leverage: "You made a bad choice. I told you the consequences, and I am following through with it."

Discussion Questions

1. Multitasking in your mind can be one of the most dangerous things you can do in your marriage. Your wife is talking, but your mind is a million miles away. How can we men change so that we actually become attentive listeners and actively engaged in

conversation with our wives instead of just shaking our heads up and down?

2. A man needs to feel respected. How well do you receive input from your wife when she talks to you about something you need to adjust?

3. Many husbands are totally unfocused on their wife's presence, failing to walk beside her, open doors for her, and to know her state of mind in public. What have you done to change that, or what needs to change about that in your marriage?

4. A child needs affirmation. Did you receive that from your father, or was he anonymous, absent, or even abusive? What have you done not to repeat that cycle with your own children? Most parents discipline in anger and frustration. How does the

idea of clear boundaries and consequences give parents all the leverage?

Ministry Time

1. Living with a wife is not easy! It takes knowledge. Most of our knowledge comes from our parents' example. Perhaps you have been through a difficult home life (fatherlessness, abuse, no discipline) and can see its effect on your being a husband and parent. Ask the group to pray for a healing to take place in your soul and for forgiveness for those who failed to give you a proper example.

2. As we covered the seven mistakes husbands make with their wives, which one of them jumped out to you as your biggest issue? Ask the group to pray for you to have a breakthrough in that area.

3. Do you have a child who exhibits signs of a lack of affirmation you may have failed to give? Share with the group about that child and let them agree with you in prayer for your child's heart to be turned back toward home.

4. It's easy to lose it when disciplining a child. If you have struggled with controlling yourself when confronting a child's will, this is a perfect moment to ask for God's grace to change you into a parent who breaks his child's will without breaking the child's spirit.

Self-Study

From the story of Adam and Eve in the Garden of Eden, we learn *that "a man shall leave his father and his mother and hold fast to his wife, and they shall become one flesh"* (Genesis 2:24).

1. *You cannot allow your parents to interfere in your marriage*

- When you say "I do," you also say good-bye to your parents' right to have any control over your marriage. You are establishing a new home and a new family, and there is no going back.

2. *Your wife is your new best friend.*

- You have to hold fast (cleave, glue) to your wife. You should do everything together, not leave her at home while you continually take off with your buddies.
- She needs your companionship, your conversation, your attention, your listening, your dating her, and your activities together.

3. *You are "one flesh" with her.*

- You are two separate people, but one flesh. This is the sexual area of marriage. Sex is merely the overflow of a deep, close relationship. It does not cover all or heal all in a marriage.

- Because you are one flesh with your wife, you can never attach yourself sexually to any other woman as long as you are biblically married to your wife.

  "Do you not know that he who is joined to a prostitute becomes one body with her? For, as it is written, 'The two will become one flesh'" (1 Corinthians 6:16).

  "Did he not make them one?...So guard yourselves in your spirit, and let none of you be faithless to the wife of your youth" (Malachi 2:15).

Action Points

1. I will seek to provide financial security, companionship, routine, communication, honor, trust, and covering for my wife. I will have an open discussion with her about these seven areas and ask her to

share with me any other areas in her life where I am not meeting her needs as a person.

2. I will attempt to spend fifteen minutes a day of quality time with each of my children in order to stay attentive to their challenges in life.

3. I will seek to affirm my children by being present at their big days, verbally congratulating them for their accomplishments, and telling them I love them daily.

4. I will lay down clear boundaries and consequences for my children and maintain those consequences when they make wrong choices.

SESSION 6

LEGACY

LISTED BELOW ARE the main points of video 6. As the video plays, fill in the blanks as that information is provided. Answers are included at the back of this guide.

I. Elijah and the Definition of Legacy

A. Elijah went up in a chariot and left behind his mantle and a ________________ __________.

1. Legacy is the process by which God takes your character, consistency, and connections to transfer kingdom values to the ________________ generation.

2. Someone is eventually going to replace you. Why would you become a model man if you were not going to try to make other model men?

B. Someone said, "From ages 0 to 30, we learn it. From 30 to 60, we earn it. From 60 and up, we ________________ it."

II. Spiritual Sons

A. *A son is a* ________________. He is a young man who accompanies you and whom you enjoy rubbing shoulders with. Legacy is not a lecture; it is a lifestyle.

B. *A son is a* ________________. He does not mind rolling up his sleeves and doing anything that you are involved in.

C. *A son is a* ________________. Never mentor anyone who will not promise you that they will mentor others.

> *"You then, my child, be strengthened by the grace that is in Christ Jesus, and what you have heard from me in the presence of many*

witnesses entrust to faithful men who will be able to teach others also" (2 Timothy 2:1-2).

III. Four Stages of Mentoring

A. ________________

1. Elijah chose Elisha.

2. Jesus chose His twelve.

B. ________________

1. Those you are mentoring need to spend time with you.

2. You will never have legacy unless you eat, walk, work, and have fun with the ones you are mentoring.

C. ________________

1. If you want to mentor someone, they have to be willing to let you confront some things in their life.

2. The will is the key. On one end of the spectrum is the strong will, and on the other is the weak will. If a man is strong willed, he needs to learn restraint,

obedience, and submission. If he is weak willed, beaten down, and passive, you have to put courage in him.

3. If a person cannot receive confrontation, he cannot become a champion.

D. ________________

1. Elisha proved his commitment when he burned his plow and killed his oxen.

2. Every person being mentored has to prove his loyalty and commitment to the person who is coaching him.

Discussion Questions

1. The post-World War II (baby boomer) generation has been known as the "me generation" because of an extreme self-focus. How has this affected the three generations that followed? What do we need to change in order to become the "mentor" generation?

____

____

2. Paul adopted Timothy as his spiritual son, his protégé, his traveling companion. He became Paul's most trusted lieutenant. Who is a man ten to twenty years younger than you who has become one of your best friends and seems to almost follow you around? What do you think he is looking for, and how are you developing him?

3. Elijah selected a young man (Elisha) who was busy plowing in the field. He chose him because he was already working hard at what he was doing. Discuss the qualities you would look for in a young man if you were to select him to be the person who would take over your life's work.

4. Confrontation is hard. Jesus had to confront His disciples, and one of them left Him. It is, however, the only way to develop champions. Who in your life has been your greatest coach, the person who developed you the most by both praise and confrontation? Share your story about that coach with the group.

Ministry Time

1. Rejection is the most terrible force in our world today. When a father figure rejects you or demeans your character in front of others, it creates a wound that may never heal. Can you remember a time when this happened to you? How have you managed to get over it? Perhaps a group member needs prayer over a personal wound that has not yet been healed.

2. Some of us have been strong willed and needed someone to harness us and direct our energies. Raise your hand if you feel you are a strong-willed person! Jesus said to God, "Not My will, but Yours be done." Let's stop a minute and pray for our wills to be totally submitted to the will of God for maximum effectiveness in our lives.

3. Some of us have lacked confidence to move forward because of a lack of coaching, mentoring, and fathering. Perhaps you were talked down to and berated all your life by authority figures. If you generally feel that something you want to do is going to fail before you even start it, raise your hand! The angel said to Gideon, *"The Lord is with you, O mighty man of valor"* (Judges 6:12) while he was hiding in the winepress. God believes in you! Let's pray for new courage and boldness to come upon us to attempt the difficult and even the impossible in our lives.

4. Pair up with one other man and talk about the natural sons or spiritual sons in your life. Pray for them and ask God to give you many sons who possess

your values and vision before you go home to be with the Lord.

Self-Study

The Bible gives us numerous examples of great mentors who developed a legacy from those who had no courage.

1. David

> *"And everyone who was in distress, and everyone who was in debt, and everyone who was bitter in soul, gathered to him. And he became the commander over them"* (1 Samuel 22:2).

- David took these four hundred men and made them into the mightiest force of men in the world. Thirty-seven of them became his "mighty men," some of whom killed over three hundred men by themselves (see 1 Chronicles 11:11).
- *Mentoring is about seeing potential.* Even though these men were in distress, in debt, and bitter, David saw in them men who

could change the world and give him the kingdom. You have to see the "sculpture in the stone," shaping and working with it until a great leader emerges.

2. *Jesus*

> *"Follow me, and I will make you fishers of men"* (Matthew 4:19).

- Jesus said, "I will *make* you." His disciples knew how to fish for fish, but they had no idea how to fish for men! His promise to them was, "If you will hang out with Me, watch Me, and do what I teach you, you will end up being great fishermen for the souls of men."
- Jesus had to confront their character, rebuke their rebuttals, and purify their pride. The disciples were rough, uneducated fishermen for the most part. These were mixed together with some political extremists and some overly spiritual leaders. *Jesus knew how to walk and work with these twelve men until they became the very foundation of the Christian church.*

3. Paul

"Be imitators of me, as I am of Christ" (1 Corinthians 11:1).

- The New Testament records twenty-three of Paul's spiritual sons who directly traveled with him and were dispatched by him to extreme parts of the Roman Empire on his behalf.

- His sons were converts who represented most of the churches he began. His team grew through the years as he picked up more and more leaders. Tradition says that Timothy, his top disciple, pastored the huge church in Ephesus.

- Paul knew just how to encourage those who were weak in their will: *"And say to Archippus: 'See that you fulfill the ministry that you have received in the Lord'"* (Colossians 4:17). Paul's disciples went to jail with him, crossed the oceans with him, walked the Roman roads with him, and were beaten with him. One of them, Philemon, met Paul in a Roman jail and was discipled into a spiritual son by him.

Action Points

1. I will focus the rest of my life on finding, training, and releasing spiritual sons who can take my values and my vision into the next generation.

2. I will determine that my integrity and character will become a model of Christ to the point that I can tell those I mentor, "Follow me, as I follow Christ." Then and only then will I be a *model man*.

ANSWER KEY

Lesson 1

II, A: *truth*

II, A, 1: *deceive*

II, A, 2: *wife*

II, B: *word*

II, B, 1: *bond*

II, B, 2: *keeping*

II, C: *bills*

II, C, 2: *tithe, taxes*

II, C, 3: *company*

II, C, 4: *correctly*

Lesson 2

I, A: *Samson*

I, B, 1: *alone*

I, B, 2: *eye*

I, B, 3: *accountable*

I, B, 4: *others*

I, B, 5: *Internet*

I, B, 6: *cable*

I, B, 7: *workplace*

II, A: *example*

II, B: *speech*

II, C: *conduct*

II, D: *order*

II, E: *family*

II, F: *children*

Lesson 3

I, A: *driven*

I, B: *with*

I, C: *ego*

I, D: *humility*

II, A: *please*

II, B: *wife*

II, C: *children*

II, D: *deserve, demand*

III, A: *margins*

III, B: *top*

III, C: *80*

IV, A: *pray*

IV, B: *open*

V, A: *schedule*

V, B: *saving*

V, C: *50*

V, D: *vacation*

V, E, 1: *eight*

V, E, 2: *2 percent*

V, E, 3: *king*

Lesson 4

I, A: *important*

I, B: *end*

I, C: *priorities*

II, A: *influence*

II, A, 3: *ambition*

II, B: *pleasing*

II, B, 3: serving

III, A: mandate

III, B: method

III, C: money

III, C, 2: vision

Lesson 5

I, A: *insecurity*

I, A, 2: *secure*

I, A, 3: *three months*

I, B: *loneliness*

I, B, 3: *disclose*

I, C: *routine*

I, D: *communication*

I, D, 2: *adjust*

I, E: *dishonor*

I, E, 3: *queen*

I, F: *mistrust*

I, G: *unprotected*

I, G, 2: *cover*

II, A: *attention*

II, B: *affection*

II, B, 3: *absent*

II, C: *discipline*

II, C, 2: *pain*

Lesson 6

I, A: *spiritual son*

I, A, 1: *next*

I, A, 3: *return*

II, A: *friend*

II, B: *servant*

II, C: *mentor*

III, A: *selection*

III, B: *impartation*

III, C: *confrontation*

III, D: *commitment*

WE WOULD LIKE TO HEAR FROM YOU:

Has this book changed your situation or given you a new perspective?

Share your story with us, review@bethanypublishing.net

Have comments for the author?

Send them to author@bethanypublishing.net

Online Resources at

www.bethanypublishing.net

Sign Up For Our Newsletter at

www.bethanypublishing.net/newsletter

To Receive Coupons, Special Offers, & Most Recent News

Be Sure To Follow Us On:

Facebook: facebook.com/Bethanypublish

Twitter: @bethanypublish

Instagram: @bethanypublishing